A GUEST OF THE WORLD

A GUEST OF THE WORLD

Meditations

Jeffrey Lockwood

SKINNER HOUSE BOOKS

BOSTON

Printed in the United States.

Cover design by Kimberly Glyder
Text design by Suzanne Morgan

ISBN 1-55896-504-1
978-1-55896-504-1

Library of Congress Cataloging-in-Publication Data

Lockwood, Jeffrey Alan, 1960-
  A guest of the world : meditations / Jeffrey Lockwood.
      p. cm.
  ISBN-13: 978-1-55896-504-1 (pbk. : alk. paper)
  ISBN-10: 1-55896-504-1 (pbk. : alk. paper) 1. Christian
life—Unitarian authors. 2. Meditations. I. Title.

BX9855.L63 2006
242—dc22

2006004608

Contents

The Fine Art of the Good Guest

The most important thing that I've learned in traveling
to more than twenty countries is the art of being a guest.
And I'm a particularly fine visitor at the supper table. I've
consumed live fish in Inner Mongolia, not-quite-coagulated
blood sausage on the Tibetan plateau, shredded pig's ear in
China, grilled lamb fat in Uzbekistan, horse steaks in Kazakh-
stan, vodka made from fermented mare's milk in Siberia,
vegemite in Australia, goat in Brazil, and snails in France. I
don't have an iron stomach, by any means, but I do have the
will to be a virtuous visitor.

We are all visitors—even when we are home. Our time in
any relationship or place is ultimately limited. We are passing
through; nobody stays forever. How might we act if we con-
sider ourselves guests in the lives of friends and family? Being
a good guest is rather simple in principle but occasionally
challenging in practice.

One begins by demanding nothing more than the bare ele-
ments of life and dignity, which every host is more than de-
lighted to exceed. The good guest then simply allows the other
person to be a good host—to share his gifts, to play her music,
to tell his stories, to show her places, and to serve his foods.
Finally, a guest should cultivate and express genuine gratitude.
It need not be effusive or exorbitant, only sincere.

We might also think of ourselves as uninvited, but not unwelcome, guests of the planet. And I think the rules for being a good guest of the world are just the same: Ask little, accept what is offered, and give thanks.

The Gift

Our Subaru Forester was sliding sideways down Interstate 80 at fifty miles per hour. My wife, Nan, had gingerly switched to the left-hand lane to avoid a truck that was overturned on the right shoulder, but no amount of experience, skill, or caution could overcome our car's mass and momentum on a nearly frictionless surface. In an instant, we'd lost traction on the icy highway and were headed toward the wide median between the east- and westbound traffic.

"We'll be all right. Just hang on," I said as Nan gripped the wheel. I figured that we might roll once we hit the grassy median, but with seatbelts and airbags we'd survive. I had time to analyze our chances because the whole event seemed to be unfolding in slow motion. As we slid into the median we didn't roll. We didn't even slow down. The sleet had glazed the grass so that we skated over sixty feet of frozen ground and headed across the oncoming lanes. Then I saw it coming.

A semi-truck was barreling toward us. I could see the driver, the silver bulldog hood ornament, the chrome grill. I rationalized that the impact wouldn't be so bad because the road was a sheet of ice; we would bounce off the truck like a hockey puck richocheting off the boards. Of course, a head-on collision would have been fatal, but I was blessedly unable to grasp my own mortality in the interminable moments as the gap closed. I winced and braced—and then came the bang.

We flattened the reflector post on the far side of the highway as the truck roared by on our right. The Subaru tilted hard to the left, then rocked to stillness. My calm detachment gave way to terror and relief. We'd cheated death by a few feet. However, it took days before I understood the gift that had been given to me.

The gift was not that we lived. Nor did I see survival as some sort of message from the Almighty about a mysterious purpose we had yet to fulfill. The physics of the world on that day simply and disinterestedly unfolded in such a way that the truck missed us. Not because we were special, or good, or called to something great, but just because when you roll the dice sometimes you get lucky. There was no greater power to thank. The meaning of the near-death experience was for me to make.

I don't believe there is a guiding hand of God shoving Subarus onto the shoulders of icy roads, but that does not mean my life has no purpose. I am part of an intractably complex world that gives me the raw material from which I am free to craft gifts and make meaning—gifts that are as authentic as life itself and meaning that is every bit as real as an oncoming truck. So, when I am trying to decide whether to take a day off to be with my family, whether my kids are now too old to kiss goodnight, whether there is time to have lunch with a colleague, whether a neighbor needs a hand clearing his yard after a windstorm, or whether to accept an awkward invitation to a dinner from a lonely acquaintance— all of which came up recently—I open my gifts.

Happiness Is a Rescued Worm

We often pine for happiness without doing something to make ourselves joyful, which is like wishing to satisfy our hunger instead of eating. But we often don't know what will make us happy. The sources of our unhappiness—friendless days, dreary jobs, uncertain finances—don't permit simple remedies. There would seem to be no single path to happiness. But every journey begins with a first step, and the initial stride is shared by many paths.

So what is this first step? The simplest act of warmth nudges us toward joy. Stroking the family cat can create this momentum for me; her purring somehow dispels the dark clouds of angst. On rainy mornings, I often scoop befuddled earthworms from the busy sidewalk and plunk them back onto the lawn. While worms would seem odd candidates for affection, their prevalence and vulnerability provide us with plentiful opportunities to relieve suffering—both ours and theirs.

When J. B. S. Haldane was asked what we can learn about God from studying His creations, the famous British scientist replied that, in light of biological diversity, the Almighty had "an inordinate fondness for beetles." Whatever the Creator's affections, tiny creatures present us with crucial choices, forks in the path of life: We can scoop up a spider rather than crushing her or shoo a fly rather than swatting him.

There are, of course, more conventional opportunities to extend a moment's tenderness in the course of a day: touch a friend, wave to a neighbor, or smile at a sales clerk. When I find myself hungering for happiness, offering a kind word to a co-worker is certainly a step in the right direction. And so is stepping over a sidewalk ant.

Hamster Wisdom

When I was a biology student, rodents were often my teachers in the laboratory. Now that I'm an adult and a teacher myself, these small creatures still provide inspiration. Indeed, I learned my greatest lesson about leadership from a hamster and a seven-year-old girl.

My daughter's first warm-blooded pet was a white dwarf hamster named Snowball. Erin found Snowball to be a wonderful companion. She was soft, intelligent, adorable, and—for the most part—affectionate. But under certain circumstances, Snowball would bite. Actually, she could be ferocious for a creature the size of a Ping-Pong ball. This is what made her a great teacher.

Snowball liked nothing better than being out of her cage, hiding in Erin's pocket, or rambling through a Hamsterville built of wooden blocks. Once she was out of her familiar—and fiercely defended—territory, Snowball flourished in the arts of exploration and mischief. The problem was how to get her from her nest into a world where she could find the love and adventure that she clearly relished. Erin could have forced Snowball into a corner, grabbed her by the scruff of the neck (as a well-meaning pet consultant suggested), and eventually broken her spirit. But some children have a wisdom that transcends brute force.

7

With patience, my daughter discovered that Snowball would readily dash into a toilet paper tube placed on the floor of her cage. Then Erin would lift the tube out of the cage, and Snowball would happily walk out onto her waiting hand. The toilet paper tube had become the hamster's bridge from the cage into the world. It allowed Snowball to maintain her dignity and sense of security while providing a transition to the warmth of a shirt pocket or the excitement of an obstacle course.

Erin learned that while it may be possible to force another being from the safety and comfort of the "known," with understanding and patience you can also find a path that allows a fearful creature to enter the larger world on its own terms. We humans like our snug cages of relationships, traditions, and rituals. But beyond the bars, mountains of possibility and oceans of experience beckon. And we are torn.

The leader's job is to find toilet paper tubes for the community —ways to enter the world without fear. It's not easy: Leaders love their cages too. And we all know that freedom comes with the risk of getting stuck between the sofa cushions, ambushed by the cat, or lost in the heater vent. But we can't let our dread of the unknown restrict what we can become.

Fishing for Answers

Living in Wyoming, I learned how to fish. With time, I came to understand that we all fish. That is, we all cast the lines of our lives into the flow of the world in the hope of hooking meaning. We are prepared to release our catch if it is small or land our quarry if it is great. As an angler, I also learned that most of the river has few fish.

One might get a nibble almost anywhere, but the chances are better if the lure drifts between the still and fast waters. The fish find little to feed on in a placid pool, and it is easy for the hook to snag on an old, sunken branch. In the rapids, the fish are tossed about and the angler finds it impossible to discern between a bite and the tugging of the current. The productive waters are where the swift current meets the quiet deep.

But a lure will not linger long in the magical space formed by a curve in the river where languid water hugs the bank and rushing water swings wide. So we must cast again and again, remaining attentive to what can be felt but not seen. Aware of the possibility of connection, we may encounter what we seek.

This is all true in my experience, but the finest fish I ever caught took my hook after a cast that landed far from the mark. I had worked my lure through what should have been perfect reaches of the river, but the long afternoon had unfolded without a nibble. That is until a wondrous creature burst from what seemed to be a shallow riffle with no promise.

A good fisherman knows where the fish might be. But, just as importantly, he recognizes that this knowledge is only the illusion that he uses to focus his awareness, to prepare himself for an encounter with the unseen. Deep within, what he truly knows is that fish—and meaning—can lurk in the most unlikely waters.

Excessive Moderation

𝒦

This evening I am going to have a grilled sausage (with sautéed peppers and onions), a big handful of kettle-fried potato chips (the really crispy ones), and a Guinness Extra Stout (a sinfully rich brew based on a formula older than America). I am paying tribute to one of the great ideas of Western civilization: moderation.

To be honest, what I'm really celebrating is having finished Aristotle's *Nicomachean Ethics*, which I cannot heartily recommend as "a good read." Even though Aristotle's son, Nicomachus, edited his work, the result is more a systematic plodding than a lively discourse. Nonetheless, the philosopher's search for happiness resonates across more than two millennia.

Aristotle proposed that authentic happiness—not mere physical satisfaction or emotional pleasure—arises from a life of virtue. But how does one attain such a life? Here the great thinker provided an answer that has shaped Western culture, religion, and values into the present day: the doctrine of the Golden Mean.

Virtue lies in avoiding excess, Aristotle said. Courage, for example, lies between cowardice and recklessness. The good life is centered, a sort of dampened equilibrium. Our government is based on a balance of powers. Wise investors maintain balanced portfolios. Nutritionists advise a balanced diet. From the myth of Icarus (whom Daedalus advised to fly the middle course between the sea and the sun) to the fairy tale of Goldilocks (who rejected the porridge that was too hot or too cold for cereal that was "just right"), stories remind us about the prudence of the middle way.

But Aristotle's advice has its own safety valve, a regulator that assures that life does not degenerate into mediocre harmony. For even moderation must be done in moderation. Should a marriage proposal or a "welcome home" hug be given halfway? Did those who supported the march from Selma or the Wilderness Act hope for a middling compromise? Where is the restraint in Beethoven's symphonies or Whitman's poems?

So I'm celebrating Aristotle's great insight with sausage, chips, and beer. Actually, I have a couple of chicken and basil sausages in the freezer rather than bratwurst. My stomach can only take so much grease, and I've found that immoderation is best in moderate doses.

We All Die, But Do We All Live?

Last fall my dad had prostate cancer and my mom had a stroke. And I learned something about fear and pride.

I was fortunate to have an older brother who lived near my folks and was able to support them. And with Dad recovering from surgery when Mom had the stroke, assistance was vital. My younger brother and sister also rallied, and I flew home as soon as I thought that I might be more of an asset than a liability. Until these crises, my parents had been remarkably healthy. We'd been on wonderfully equal footing; visits were a matter of sharing lives rather than giving care.

I don't dwell on death, but for some time I've been coming to terms with my own mortality. Maybe middle age—a sort of statistical halfway point in life—provokes such reflection. My aunt died a year ago and friends in their seventies have died recently, so I'd contemplated my parents' mortality. Even though I've been on my own for a quarter century, I admit to a puzzling sense of loneliness, almost homelessness, when I think of my mom and dad dying. While their illnesses brought these feelings into focus, this sense of mortality was not what transformed my sense of the world.

The changes associated with growing children and aging parents hardly make for an original story. Self-help books and television talk shows are filled with members of "the sandwich generation" having to care for children and parents at the same time. We hear about the physical demands, financial strains, emotional trials, and spiritual depletions of caretakers. I expect that my obligations will increase in the coming years. But for now, my reordered world is an unexpected gift. I'm focusing not on being worried but on being proud.

For forty-five years, Mom and Dad have expressed their joy in my accomplishments, just as I've relished the successes of my own children. I'd never thought much about what my parents had achieved until my mom's stroke. Immediately afterward, she was unable to speak, to lift her right arm, to grasp an object, or to stand, let alone walk. Rehabilitation was exhausting, tedious, and frustratingly incremental, but Dad was there for her and she wouldn't quit. Today she's talking, walking, driving— and planning to visit Spain and Morocco this summer.

They had traveled the world for years, and a trip to Eastern Europe was scheduled when illness struck. I know they thought about what might have happened if they'd been abroad, and I wondered whether a sense of vulnerability would deter them in the future. We've not talked about such matters. That's not how my family works. We don't have soul-wrenching sessions of sharing; we allow our lives to speak for us.

What I'm hearing is that as you get older, you don't fear dying—you fear not living. The French philosopher Jean-Jacques Rousseau asked, "Is the moment when we have to die the time to learn how we should have lived?" Mom and Dad have answered this with a courageous no. I'm proud of them. And just a little worried.

Trash Can Blessings

The most public prayer in our society is found in the most unlikely place—trash cans. Throughout our country, the swinging flaps of garbage bins say, "Thank you." Of course, the intent is to express gratitude for putting trash in the container rather than on the ground. But there may be a deeper meaning: a prayer of thanksgiving that could change the world, one napkin at a time.

What if the thanks is not for your decision to refrain from littering but for the trash itself? Japanese Buddhism reminds us that all things matter; even mundane objects have a purpose. This insight gives rise to the custom of *kuyo*, a ceremony of gratitude for all that we have used.

We can think of *kuyo* as an expression of deep materialism, consumption done well. From this perspective, we might see the trash can as a sacred vessel and the "thank you" on its lid as a call for *kuyo*. With this in mind, I pause and acknowledge the napkin's gift to me of cleanliness. Then I extend my gratitude to the tree from which the napkin was made. Even a moment of thanks is worthwhile, for frequency of prayer is more important than duration.

Of course, I often forget to give thanks to my garbage, but I'm getting better at it. In matters of prayer, one need only seek improvement, not perfection. So now, when I begin to grab a few napkins, I stop for a moment. The blessing printed on the flap of the container nearby reminds me to give thanks to the paper and the tree. And I decide that one napkin should be plenty for my desires—and perhaps more than enough for my needs.

Playful Protest

Every Wednesday morning I join a friend in a public protest at a downtown coffee shop. In defiance of social norms we play chess instead of going to our jobs. For an hour or so, Mike and I refuse to work; we play openly, in the midst of the economic machinery of modern society. Two reasonably bright, well-paid, highly educated men—with jobs to do, e-mails queuing, phone message lights flashing, and meetings pending—play a game. To make our two-person demonstration still more radical, we devised a subversive rule: Last week's winner has to buy the coffee. This regular sit-in might seem a bit trivial in the grand scheme, but not working turns out to be remarkably challenging.

Not a week goes by in which I don't wonder if I really have the time for play in the midst of deadlines and demands. And I know that Mike, working for an understaffed nonprofit agency, is in the same position. Either of us could easily cancel the game with a quick e-mail, and we'd both feel a momentary sense of comfort at having Wednesday morning available to finish a report or refine a presentation. Like addicts getting a fix, we would feel a flush of relief as the drug called work coursed through our bodies. Our society encourages workaholism—a destructive compulsion that consumes our lives as we pursue productivity.

For years I tried to set aside bits of time during the week for reading, exercising, or other useful distractions. But I always failed. I wasn't planning to bilk the system; I typically worked through lunch and often put in fifty or sixty hours a week. A few hours of sanctuary amid the flurry of meetings, lectures, and experiments would have been reasonable. But the whirlpool of demands invariably sucked me back into vain promises that I'd set aside the time next week. Breaking the habit of work required more self-discipline than I had. To succeed I needed a partner, a co-conspirator.

Mike and I didn't set out to become protestors. We started playing chess when he was struggling with some tough personal matters and it seemed that spending a bit of time together was the best thing I could do for him. This initial decision, to place a person above work, turned into a habit of the heart. I don't know if I helped Mike much during his difficult time, but he's made me understand that people are more lovable than work. When pressures build, I still feel the whirlpool tugging at me. But now I see that, rather than being too busy to play, I am too busy not to.

Chess is our methadone, the activity that substitutes for work. Early on, I even rationalized that the mental discipline of the game made me more productive. These days, the game is less important. Not because of my losing record as Mike might contend (he buys the coffee three out of four weeks), but because we both understand that the game is the means to an end. It is the protest sign we hold up, knowing that the real reason for our revolutionary action is to be together. To work—at least for a few hours—on being human.

The Labor of Living

In math I was admonished to "show my work," and in English I had to turn in my rough drafts. As a student, these seemed like perverse requirements. What difference did it make how I arrived at the correct algebraic solution or the well-crafted paragraph? Now that I'm a professor, I appreciate the value of seeing the labor that goes into a final product. A colleague in engineering once told me that such an approach smacked of making excuses: "In engineering there is no partial credit. You don't get paid half of a contract if you build a bridge that collapses under half of the specified load." Fair enough. There's something to be said for standards.

But another reason for seeing the work that went into the essay or equation is that it tells me what went wrong. If I'm a good enough teacher, I can help the student avoid the error in the future. What's more, I can see the student's effort and decide how to allocate my time among those needing help. It sounds callous, but it's quite the opposite. Witnessing the struggle of my students has deepened my compassion.

Early on, as a naive assistant professor, I told my students that I'd match their efforts at learning with my own at teaching. I imagined that their shortcomings were invariably due to a lack of self-discipline, a mental laziness, a failure to devote themselves to scholarship. Often I was right. But in time I learned that when I was wrong, I was tragically wrong. I realized that I will never be able to match the blood, sweat, and tears shed by many of my students in their pursuit of learning and life.

I've come to know the schizophrenic pupil, who managed to learn while his mind wrestled with insane thoughts muffled by psychotropic drugs, and the sleepy-eyed student, who was not a party animal but rather a single father nursing his feverish child after the mother walked out on them. A young woman arrived in my classroom late and out of breath, not because she was irresponsible but because she'd been battling through a heart-pounding anxiety attack that left her gasping for air as she left her apartment. One student, who had escaped the suffocating smallness of her rural high school, fought the urge to drown her insecurities in alcohol while holding back tears of frustration with the problems I assigned. Another young scholar had abdominal pains that were so agonizing that her mind alternated between my reading assignment and thoughts of suicide. She was eventually forced to drop out of school and was later diagnosed with a rare intestinal disorder.

What if everyone showed their work? What if I knew how much struggle that waitress had gone through during exhausting weeks of relearning to walk after a stroke? Or how much turmoil went into the bookkeeper's efforts to leave her house without checking the door dozens of times in the grip of an obsessive-compulsive disorder? Or how much gut-wrenching anxiety went into a co-worker's battle to begin his day without that pill, powder, or injection? I might be willing to leave the waitress a generous tip despite mixed-up orders, to overlook a mistyped purchase order, or to wait patiently for a reply to an unanswered e-mail.

But I have to maintain some standard of performance and adhere to a minimal measure of quality—right? Or maybe, if I knew the labors of other lives, I'd apply that standard of performance to my own humanity and that measure of quality to my own soul.

To Ask Is to Give

A voice screeched gate assignments through a nerve-jangling public address system. Even if the announcements had been in English, I doubt that I'd have been able to make sense of them. But whatever was being broadcast to the cavernous waiting area of the Moscow airport prompted mobs of people to head toward the buses that shuttled passengers to the planes. I grew panicky as I realized that there was no chance of figuring out which announcement concerned my flight. Staring desperately at my boarding pass, I realized that all I had to do was find a Russian with a matching flight number and follow him. To my right was a morose old fellow whose pass was tucked into the pocket of his threadbare suit coat. To my left was salvation.

A pretty teenager had her boarding pass stuck in the book she was reading, and the first two digits of her flight number were the same as mine. Hoping to see the numbers hidden by the edge of the page, I carefully leaned over. Sensing my movement, she turned to look at me. I pointed hopefully at my boarding pass and then at hers. To my relief, she immediately understood. But we'd attracted the attention of her parents and younger brother. When she explained my situation, her mother smiled warmly and launched into what I took to be an offer to help. I nodded, correctly guessing that I'd been temporarily adopted.

When our flight was announced, the mother leapt to her feet and grasped me by the elbow. She ushered me toward the gate, shouting directions to the others, as the boy grabbed my backpack and the girl and her father hauled the rest of the luggage. The mother pushed through the crowd, returning scowls with her own glare and dragging me along until we'd boarded the bus. Once at the plane, I thanked her profusely, using one of the few Russian words I knew. She seemed to thank me in return. But why would she be grateful?

One of the great blessings of travel is to be put in a position of asking help from others, to be genuinely needful of strangers. Our illusion of self-reliance evaporates as the unexpected and the unfamiliar merge into vulnerability. We offer the gift of authentic need, the opportunity for deep trust. We express to another person the most humanizing cross-cultural phrase: "Please, help me."

Many of the most meaningful times in my life have been when others have invited me into their lives, allowing me to help. Often it has been simply to point toward a landmark, demonstrate how to use a pay phone, or show the way on a map. Sometimes the aid has been more elaborate—endorsing an application for permanent residency or providing a letter of support for political asylum. I've also seen travelers who have become lost within themselves. Frightened students have shared their depression, delusion, or dependency with me, and I've led them to the mental health center on campus to begin their journey back to wholeness.

In our society, self-sufficiency is heralded as a virtue, and chronic dependence on others can be degrading. But never being asked to help another person is isolating, even dehumanizing. In a culture that exalts autonomy, asking for help may be one of the greatest gifts we can offer. So much of life has become a calculation of costs and benefits; to ask assistance is to create the opportunity for unconditional giving in raw, spiritual defiance of economic rationality. We become mutually indebted without expectation of repayment. Each person in the relationship becomes both a giver and a receiver. Each one becomes more human. Each one has something to be thankful for.

For the Love of Stuff

※

If materialism is the scourge of spiritual enlightenment, then few experiences hold less potential for deep meaning than buying a car—or so it seemed to me before I began the venture. The most difficult aspect should have been paying more for a car than my parents paid for their first house. But I was surprised to find that the real challenge was giving up our 1980 Datsun 210 station wagon with its cracked vinyl seats disgorging hunks of foam.

We fondly nicknamed the jalopy Green Car, referring to its oxidizing color. The mechanic had told me some months earlier that the front end had deteriorated to the point that driving on the highway was suicidal, and since then the car had further accentuated its chronic desire to turn right. My wife and I bought Green Car in our first year of graduate school in Louisiana, where the rust problem began. The car is full of memories, like the peeling LSU decal on the back window and the broken door of the glove box that a dear friend inadvertently shattered on a bitterly cold day.

When the time finally came to admit that we needed a new car, I realized the obvious: A car is a really big thing. This wasn't a great insight, but throwing out a big thing made me think about all of the human labor and natural resources that went into it. And so arose my dilemma.

I deplore both materialism and our throwaway society, but if "stuff" doesn't matter, then what's wrong with throwing it away? Perhaps what we need is not less affection for stuff but a *deeper* attachment to material goods in order to truly see how our things connect us to the earth, life, and people. There was a spiritual side to Green Car: the gouge in the earth from which its iron was extracted, the holes in the oceans from which its fuel was pumped, the ancient life forms that were converted into its plastics, the engineers who devised its components, the friends it transported, and the places it took us. As a society of users and consumers, we take what we can and give what we must; we don't have time for sentimental attachments to old cars, old books, or old people. Avoiding connections makes it easier to create trash, throwaway people, and disposable relationships.

So in the end we didn't consign Green Car to the junkyard. Green Car is helping a friend, Dennis, who needs transportation around town. When I look at the bathroom fittings and thermostat that Dennis installed in exchange, a new strand appears in my life. Moreover, I know that the jalopy and the handyman will get along. After all, both have a tendency to avoid straight paths, although one tends to the literal right and the other to the political left. Both are dependable but not entirely predictable. And both are connected to me.

Raffle Wisdom

Life is a chancy affair, a sort of cosmic game of dice. I'm quite familiar with games of chance. It's not that I gamble in Las Vegas and I've never bought a lottery ticket, but I'm the ultimate sucker for kids selling raffle tickets. When the doorbell rings, my wife shoos me away. Otherwise, she knows we'll end up with pancake breakfast tickets, chocolate bars, or magazine subscriptions. When it comes to charitable causes, Nan is actually more generous than I am, but she's more discerning. I've bought raffle tickets when the winning prize was a rifle, and I don't hunt or even want a gun in the house. (But the little fellow was raising money for a scout trip.) I'm not much better at resisting the Shriners, VFW, or the Police Athletic League, so Nan also tries to keep me from answering the phone around dinnertime. She pretends that my inability to turn down raffle tickets drives her crazy, but I know that deep down she finds it endearing that I'm a softy.

I don't enter raffles believing that I'll win. I've come to think of the tickets as an inadvertent lesson about life. At least, I'm pretty sure that most raffles are not designed to provide a deep message. But being something of an unwitting connoisseur of raffle tickets, I've come to realize that often they include an unexpectedly compelling insight. On one side is a string of numbers, reflecting the utter arbitrariness with which the world seems to unfold. There might also be a list of prizes, the items that can be won with a bit of luck. I prefer raffles with lots of small prizes rather than a single big one; I'm not sure whether I really want a convertible, and little things can make wonderful surprises without demanding insurance and taxes.

But the real insight is printed on the back of the ticket, where few people bother to look. Raffle tickets warn us, "You must be present to win." In life, showing up is often half the battle. But of course, simply being somewhere physically is not the same as being present. I don't know how many drawings I might have won if I'd been present. But I do know that if life is a raffle, you can't possibly win if you're not there—if you're regretting yesterday or planning for tomorrow and the drawing is today, if you're working one evening and your child happens to pick that night to share his dreams, if you're watching television and the night sky is presenting the northern lights or a meteor shower.

There's no guarantee that your number will be drawn, even if you *are* present, but if you're fully aware, the list of prizes on the front of the ticket becomes enormous. Of course, there may not be a grand prize—more often life's raffle seems to promise lots of little things. But then, I've always favored raffles with lots of small prizes.

Quiet Eloquence

A universally accepted educational principle says that the ideal time to learn languages is while you are young. We might endlessly debate the best way to teach math, the surest method for conveying grammar, or the optimal way to engage students in science and art, but when it comes to languages, nearly everyone agrees that the sooner one starts, the better. There is an exception to this rule, however. One language is so difficult to learn that we must mature before even making an attempt. And despite countless hours of drill, most adults fail to master it. We find it hard to be silent.

I had the requisite year of French in high school, three semesters of German in college, and in my travels I've temporarily grasped some useful phrases in Chinese, Portuguese, Russian, and Spanish. But I never struggled as mightily with these languages as I have with my newest subject. Silence is the most alien of tongues. The vocabulary couldn't be simpler and there are no rules of pronunciation, grammar, or tense to memorize, but silence is the hardest language to put into practice. Henry Adams claimed that he never labored so hard to learn a language as he did to hold his tongue.

For more than forty years I have argued, suggested, ranted, pontificated, protested, and lectured. These forms of speech have often served me well, but sometimes—too often—they have led to conflict, misunderstanding, and hurt. Gradually,

I am learning that silence can be more effective. Holding my tongue is especially appropriate in response to angry words, impetuous insults, rash accusations, unintended slurs, disingenuous flattery, and painful stories. It is also powerful while on a long drive with a close friend, walking a familiar path with a lover, gardening on a summer morning with a daughter, or fishing a mountain stream with a son.

Like any language, silence can be misinterpreted and misused. An icy quiet can be a way of hurting those who long for our words. A wordless evening allows us to avoid a difficult subject. But some problems that appear so enormous that they demand immediate airing crumble to insignificance with the perspective of a few quiet hours. I have often wished that I had not rushed to speak but seldom regretted waiting in silence.

I greatly admire my multilingual friends, but in middle age I've largely abandoned the idea of mastering French or German. I like to think that while learning new languages might be a gift of youth, wordlessness could be a grace of maturity. Knowing how and when to be quiet is a demanding task. But with practice it may be possible to become fluent in silence.

Who Cares?

In our modern age of apathy and egoism, there is cause for hope whenever people care about something beyond themselves. But there is more to being human than feeling deeply, for we risk becoming impassioned fools. Our minds must conspire with our hearts. We should care enough to think— and think with great care.

No human endeavor shows the double-edged nature of caring like religion, with its boundless capacity to foster our humanity and its vulnerability to thoughtless passion. In a world of suffering, to devote our spiritual energy to theological trifles is not just absurd, it is immoral. Yet we persist, as if such details mattered.

Who cares whether Jesus was divine if we treat the homeless man in the alley as less than human?

Who cares whether God is omnipotent if we don't use our power to help others?

Who cares whether the Bible's authors were divinely inspired if we write laws that are profane?

Who cares whether there is a heaven if the hell of domestic violence burns next door?

Who cares whether Mary was a virgin if we do not heed the cries of a woman being raped?

Who cares whether we are saved when a child loses all hope?

Who cares whether the earth was created in seven days if seventy species disappear every day?

The answer is, of course, that many people care about religious matters. And perhaps care, like love, is not a finite resource. Maybe some people have such a capacity for caring that worries about God don't detract from their concern for people. But I am not so blessed. So, for everyone else like me, let us try to build a life in which we care about the things that matter most.

A Warm Spot

Curled beneath a thin, woolen blanket not quite long enough to reach from chin to toes, I was shivering in the penetrating dampness of early spring in a drafty farmhouse on New Zealand's south island. A gray drizzle hushed the world.

My host, having cleaned up the kitchen and tended to the animals, tapped on my door on his way to bed and peeked in, holding a hot water bottle. Had God appeared bearing the keys to the pearly gates, I could not have been more thankful. As the heat flowed into my body from that flabby rubber bag, I recalled my journey and the power of another kind of warmth.

The flight to New Zealand had been arduous—a hectic scramble to make a connection in Los Angeles, an insipid dinner on the plane, and a shivering night of sporadic sleep in a sitting position. I don't know why international flights are gradually cooled during transit, but halfway through the journey I was freezing. What stood out vividly in my memory was a stewardess who saw my battle against the cold. In the middle of the night she brought me a blanket.

The airlines remind us that the flight attendants are concerned primarily with our safety, not our comfort. I'm sure that my blanket-bearer was not expected to walk the aisles in search of shivering passengers. While her small act of kindness did not take any great effort, did not involve a Mother Teresa sort of sacrifice or heroic courage, it was also not necessary. She cared enough to notice my discomfort and provide a bit of warmth amid the icy disinterest of modern travel. This was the zenith of my trek, the only moment in a blurred voyage that remains as a clear memory.

To warm our bodies and spirits, we do not need to be immersed in a hot tub or bathed in kindness. The hot water bottle covered a few square inches, and the stewardess's act took a few moments. In the cold reality of the modern world, a heartfelt smile, a door held open, or a sincere "thank you" may be the packet of warmth that another person presses to his chest to feel comfort on a soul-chilling day.

The Fair Fight

Bullies are a serious problem in our schools. But current programs to prevent bullying seem to cast too wide a net by implicating violence as the problem. For violence—like pain and death—is a part of being in the world. The real issue, as I learned in fifth grade, is fairness.

A bully picks on those who are vulnerable, victims who can be easily defeated. I remember getting throttled while playing basketball against older boys at the Catholic school that my older brother, Steve, and I attended. Ronnie, one of the eighth-graders, took cheap shots during the game, intimidating me because I'd blocked his shot in the opening minutes. At half-time, Steve walked up to Ronnie and shoved him in the chest, knocking him against a chain-link fence. "Cut it out" was all he said—and Ronnie knew exactly what he meant.

Also in fifth grade I had a series of run-ins with Brian, a red-headed, trash-talking fireball in my own class. He was tough and intimidated me thoroughly. Finally, I'd had enough, and the two of us squared off on the playground. Such events invariably drew a crowd, including the older boys. We flailed away at each other with the typical ineptitude of kids; I received a bloody nose and tore my shirt. Steve didn't come to my rescue because it was a fair fight, and to step in might have saved my nose but would have cost my dignity. Nobody likes a bully, but it's hard to respect a wimp.

Neither Ronnie nor Brian ever picked on me again. The lesson I took away as a ten-year-old kid was not the role of violence in human affairs but the importance of fairness. The eighth-grader would have throttled me, and Steve knew that was unjust. But my classmate probably wasn't going to do any serious harm, so I was expected to hold my own, to stand up for myself.

When we deplore violence, we take on a challenge of cosmic proportions. Do we really want to ban the tactic of taking a charge or setting a hard pick in basketball, or do we actually want players to have a fair chance in terms of their size and skills? When we deplore suffering, do we want an immortal existence free of infection and disease, or do we really seek a just distribution of food and medicine?

The answers matter because bullies grow up, and we must choose our moral battles—as well as our physical fights—wisely. Worldwide disarmament is a fine goal, but what shall we do about conflicts in the meantime? Perhaps I'm being anachronistic, but at least some of what I really need to know I learned in the fifth grade.

While we aspire to nonviolent resolutions of human conflict, I wonder how things would change if we just settled for fair fights. Superpowers looking for an excuse to drop their arsenals on weak nations and terrorists planting bombs on trains carrying civilians are deplorable acts of bullying. I suspect that given the prospects of a fair fight, military, political, and religious leaders would be far less inclined to use violence—particularly if they themselves had to do the fighting.

Try Being Me

The most difficult part of being a professor is telling students that they can't be what they want to be. Although a student can engage the world in a vast range of ways, the reality that she cannot be something in particular comes as a blow. But I owe my students both honesty and compassion, even if others have told them the great cultural lie: You can be anything you want to be. The truth is that you can't. But what if you could?

If I could be anything, then perhaps I'd be a major league baseball player (a shortstop for the Dodgers, to be precise), or a Nobel laureate (either Peace or Literature, or maybe both, if anything's possible). If I could be anything I set my mind to, the only reason for failure would be a lack of discipline, desire, and character—whatever I was would be a matter of pure whimsy. There would be no search for an authentic path; every outcome would be equally plausible. I would never feel called to anything other than whatever venture satisfied a capricious urge. But I can't be anything. And that is good.

I can be many different things, and some ways of making my way in the world will surely be smoother than others. And I can change. But I am someone, not just anyone. I was born into a story crafted by evolution, society, family, and authors I have yet to know. It is not a script but a tale of where I've come from, a story that must be honored as I write my own chapter. Genetics assured that I would not be a world-class sprinter (bad knees); society assured that I would not be a headhunter (legal constraints); and family assured that I would not be a rabbi (Catholic upbringing).

We find it difficult to accept that we are limited in our journey. But if there are no footprints behind and there is no path ahead, we wander aimlessly. We are free to be anywhere but are perpetually nowhere. The liberal tradition yearns for unconditional freedom, but how valuable is a blank book into which anything may be written? If you could be anything, truly anything at all, then you could be me or I could be you. We would be impulsively penciled characters in meaningless fables. Erased and rewritten at will, our stories would come from nowhere and matter to nobody.

The struggle of being human is to grope with one hand, feeling and probing the limits of our lives. And with our other hand, we hold fast to another person on the path—an ancestor, a parent, a child, a friend, a spouse, or a teacher. A teacher who might go with us into the dark forest of self-doubt where we fear to step off the path that others have laid. Most of my students fail a course of study that was mapped out for them by their parents or society. And for every time that I must tell a student that he cannot be something that he believed had been fated, there are ten opportunities to show others that they can be something more than they'd imagined possible.

Ordering Avocado Sandwiches

❧

"Deluxe avocado again?" my wife asked incredulously. We don't go out for lunch very often, but my favorite place is Jeffry's Bistro and my favorite sandwich is the deluxe avocado. I'd dutifully scanned the menu, considered the options, and settled on my usual. I gave a wan smile, and Nan suggested, "You're in a rut."

"How come," I replied, "being married for eighteen years is virtuous but ordering the same lunch is a character flaw?"

"Being faithful to me is not the same as sticking with avocado sandwiches," she said.

"I like to think that I'm just a constitutionally loyal sort of person," I responded

That was nearly a decade ago, and I'm still ordering the deluxe avocado sandwich, still married—and still wondering whether I'm in a rut.

Why are change and variation so celebrated? What's wrong with regularity? There are certainly enough medicines extolling its virtues. What if our bodies, our minds, and our hearts functioned willy-nilly? We'd never know what to expect. Patterns give our lives a familiar framework. Through repetition we cultivate *familia*, literally, a household. Through constancy of people and places, we shape a sanctuary in a chaotic world. At ten in the morning I have coffee with my co-workers, and at five in the afternoon I go to the gym and sweat with a steadfast group of middle-aged guys. I like the sense of dependability, safety, and assurance that comes with these rituals.

We can become slaves to custom, and fears of bondage seem to drive the modern disdain for traditions. We see earlier people as mindless adherents to cultural norms. When our patterns of life become thoughtless and we are disconnected from the meaning of our actions, we are enslaved. But from what do we seek to be liberated? If we have no traditions, we are free to dismiss the holidays as being insignificant and go about our work. If there are no rituals, we are released from the deep meaning in our actions. If there are no customs, we are free to welcome people into a community devoid of a meaningful story. But there is a middle way.

By choosing a pattern in our lives, by understanding how it binds us to our community and our past, and by allowing it to soothe our minds, bodies, and souls, we transform a mere habit into a sacred rite. We cultivate a sense of continuity and connectedness. We shape our home in the world. So what about my deluxe avocado sandwich?

Over the years, Nan and I have developed a stylized and predictable dialogue about my lunch selection; it's a sort of ritual. I know that after perusing the menu, Nan will give me an expectant look. I'll shrug and say, "The deluxe avocado." She'll give me a half smile and shake her head in mock disgust at my lack of originality. Then I'll say, "Loyalty's a good thing." And we both know that I don't mean the sandwich.

Fatigues

Men and women wearing desert camouflage have become fixtures in major airports. The ebb and flow of soldiers has become like the breath of the nation, exhaling our youth into Iraq and inhaling the survivors back home. The soldiers look tired, fatigued.

Fatigue. This name for the standard issue uniform originally alluded to the menial labor that characterized a soldier's day—cleaning latrines, standing watch, filling sandbags. In wartime, the notion of fatigues became even more apropos; exhausting days alternated with sleepless nights, and the troops became bone tired. In the early 1980s, the military began to call this everyday wear "battle dress uniforms," as if one dressed for killing the way one dressed for dinner. Last year, the military supplanted this term with the less euphemistic "army combat uniform." We should return to "fatigues," for this is the essence of the ongoing war.

As I write this, our nation has spent $251 billion in the fight, enough to have provided health care for 57 million people or to have built more than two million affordable housing units. After thirty-five months of being bombarded by images of suffering, we are worn out. After 151 weeks of being assailed by rationalization and deceit, we are drained. After 1,057 days of being besieged by tales of torture, the nation is exhausted.

We are weary of digging ever deeper into debt,

    weary of car bombs ripping apart innocent lives,

    weary of the killing done in our name,

    weary of waiting for the next September 11th,

    weary of needless suffering,

    weary of hubris.

Fatigued.

Hear! Hear!

This summer, I'm on a personal crusade to save a dying art. It's quite a noble venture on my part, given that I will receive no material compensation. However, a puritanical work ethic would suggest that my campaign is wasting time that might be better spent fixing the leaky plumbing in the laundry room. But the Puritans were never connoisseurs of major league baseball.

Professional sport is not, of course, the languishing skill to which I refer. I am resuscitating the art of listening by following baseball on the radio. I'd like to claim that my virtuous efforts are grounded in a voluntary commitment to reviving the most human of the arts, but the actual reason is that our local reception is sketchy at best and we don't want to spend money on cable television. It is sometimes possible to get a picture on the television, but then the sound is pure static. So I follow the Colorado Rockies—an act of ascetic devotion in itself—by listening to Jeff Kingery and Jack Corrigan on KOA. There is a good reason that I prefer to listen rather than watch.

As a kid, I used to go to sleep in the summer listening to the radio broadcast of the Triple-A Albuquerque Dukes. Having spent a fair number of evenings at the ballpark, I could picture the game as the play-by-play and color announcers described the action. Today, our information is so intensely visual that authentic listening is a quaint anachronism. This would be fine except for one thing—we are still storytellers.

I'm genuinely encouraged by the surging sales of audio books, for it affirms our continuing passion for stories. Some pundits criticize these recordings as chipping away at our ability to read. They are right to be concerned, but there is a skill even more vital than literacy. Let us call it "listenacy"—the capacity to truly receive and deeply engage the human voice. Perhaps many of the world's problems would be addressed if more people could read, but in the industrial nations, at least, I wonder how many problems arise because we can't listen. Few conflicts have arisen because people failed to read the writings of one another, but much blood has been shed because we failed to listen to what others were saying.

The spoken word is a million years old, the written word but five thousand. The stories of our cultures, communities, and families were told long before they were written down. We know in a deep sense that to truly hear another person is an intimate act, joining speaker and listener. We take in the human voice and from it create a world that is an expression of two lives.

There is a good reason that I prefer to hear the baseball game on the radio rather than watch it on television or, for that matter, read the box scores in the paper. It is the same reason that ministers speak to us from the pulpit when we could just as well read their sermons. The reason that husbands and wives call each other when they might otherwise send an e-mail. And the reason I tell my children that I love them when they go to bed when I could just write a note and post it on the headboard.

Life Giving

Making a small purchase at a Disney World gift shop hardly seemed like a transformative act. Nonetheless, I came back from a meeting in Orlando with the first gift for my first child, although she was not due for another seven months. When my wife called after her checkup a couple weeks later, there was anguish in her voice, a pain I'd never heard before. I raced home from work and tried to make sense of the diagnosis: missed abortion—a dead fetus retained in the womb.

We embraced and cried for ourselves, each other, and the life we had lost. My grandfathers passed away when I was young, a good friend died suddenly in my sophomore year of college, and another friend was killed in a car accident shortly after graduation. I'd been shocked and saddened, but my first encounter with authentic grief came with the loss of a life I'd never met.

Gentle voices tried to comfort us with reminders that the fetus must not have been healthy, that this potential child was not meant to be. But the child was not hypothetical—its life had been made real by a mother falling in love with the being in her womb. And by a father's act of affirmation, a Jiminy Cricket doll tucked away in a closet.

In a high school anthropology class, I'd learned that some African tribes do not name their babies until a year after birth to avoid affirming new lives in cultures with high infant mortality. At the time, this practice seemed absurdly contrived. Now I understand.

I know the power of acknowledging life and the staggering responsibility of the living. To allow a new life into your heart is a mystical rite, a sacrament, a communion. I know now that life is made real by the living.

No More

~~

When I was a kid, I fought the demon of an emerging obsessive-compulsive disorder. I was so ashamed of this weakness, of the utter absurdity of my battle, that I never shared it with another person. I doubt anyone in my family was aware of my struggle to stop my mind from forcing me into irrational actions.

Here's how it worked. Sitting alone quietly, I'd happen to scratch my cheek, rub my nose, or touch my leg with my left hand. That seemed normal enough. But then I'd have to match the movement with my right hand. I was compelled to mirror the two halves of my body, to maintain a perfect equilibrium, down to the finest movement. I'd try to sit perfectly still, but then my right eye would twitch or my left foot would shift, and the counterbalancing move was compulsory.

The great American philosopher and psychologist William James once suggested that "when a person has an inborn genius for certain emotions, his life differs strangely from that of ordinary people." Viewed in this light, depression is a genius for hopelessness, psychosis a genius for imagination, and schizophrenia a genius for alternative views. Although long outmoded, James's insight sheds a compassionate light on our inner struggles and resonates with my experience. Perhaps my obsessive-compulsive quality represented a genius for regularity and attention to detail. With time, I discovered a means of breaking the cycle and having my "genius" work for, rather than against, me.

I found that if I simply said half aloud and repeated, "No more," I could break the spell and regain control. For thirty years, I've not found it necessary to conjure up sanity in this way. I like my tidy desk, but I feel no anxiety about having a messy garage. And when a flurry of sudden demands creates an oppressive need to impose order, I take a walk. This digression would seem to simply put me further behind, but my walk is a defiant act—a sort of ambulatory incantation, as if to say "No more." I can then return to my day with a sense of order that is empowering, not destructive.

But I wonder about other forms of madness creeping into my life. Today's world seems obsessed with security and safety, compelled by health and wealth. We cannot have too much homeland defense, insurance, technology, or savings. There is no such thing as too many diagnostic tests, warning labels, prisons, or products. A sense of debilitating irrationality descends over us as we confront our own physical limits. We are drawn into crazed desires that cannot be fulfilled. Our genius for insecurity and acquisition drives a strange cycle of anxiety and consumption.

Perhaps we need a social incantation to bring us back into balance, to break the spell of fear and greed. There is no magical tonic for the soul, but when I feel myself being crushed between the jaws of worry and greed, I want to regain control. Having had a bit of practice, I've found that a simple prayer can restore sanity. It goes like this: "No more."

Believing Is Seeing

The prairie is ecstatic this spring. Literally. I didn't say, "The prairie looks like a jubilant foal." That would be a simile—and a rather bad one at that. Nor do I intend to use "ecstatic" as a metaphor. I mean that, having spent twenty years on the steppes of Wyoming, the last six in the midst of a drought, I have seen the spring rains bring jubilation to the land. Not something like joy but real joy—the same joy that fills me when I see the green hills bursting with vitality. This elation is not merely a projection of myself. It is the prairie's joy. What foolishness, you say. How can one know the land in this way?

Autistic individuals cannot perceive the dispositions of others. They cannot make the connection between a smile on a person's face and that person's emotional state. It's not that they don't see the smile. But they don't make the connection between the smile and happiness. With extensive therapy, some autistic children can be taught to systematically make these connections, but it seems that the associations never become intuitive. The autistic person can be convinced that a smile means that another person is joyful, but this is because we insist that this is what normal people understand to be the case.

Perhaps most of us are autistic to the moods of the natural world. Maybe those who occasionally glimpse the ecstasy of the prairie, the smile of a birch, or the weeping of a mountain actually see nature like "normal" people see one another. I don't perceive the anxiety of the redwoods, but I don't live in California. I haven't spent years in ancient forests. But others have, and they say that the trees are apprehensive. Maybe they are charlatans—people who exploit the mysteries of the world for their own empowerment and gain. Perhaps they have a political agenda or want to start an eco-psychic hotline. ("Hello. This is Miss Cleo, and I can tell that your lawn is depressed. That'll be $24.99, but for another $4.95 I'll read the mental state of your geranium.")

But what if there were poets, mystics, and shamans who perceive in ways that the rest of us only experience in unbidden moments of understanding? My radical claim of prairie joy comes from a fleeting experience while walking on the grassland with my daughter in early June—just the two of us, going nowhere, being together. I was listening wholeheartedly to her, receptive in a way that is all too rare in the midst of daily life. She was sharing her feelings about the windswept Laramie valley, how happy she was to share this austere place with a new friend from overseas, how she might sometimes criticize the emptiness of this land but she'd defend its beauty to outsiders, how the prairie was like her younger brother—she could pick on Ethan, but woe to anyone else who insulted him. Then, for a moment, I knew the grassland was listening, that the three of us were happy.

No, not just happy. Ecstatic.

The Damper Pedal

I've long enjoyed the hymn "Where Is Our Holy Church?"
Some of my affection has to do with the song's one-octave
range according with the limits of my voice. But I also find
the lyrics compelling. The answer to the question raised in
the song's title is, "where race and class unite, as equal per-
sons in the search for beauty, truth, and right."

The quest for meaning in life is often a matter of seeking
these ideals. As a scientist, I'm supposed to know the truth
about the world. And as a teacher of ethics, students expect
that I have insight as to what is right. But given my artistic
talents, it would seem best if I left aesthetics to the experts.
However, I sometimes believe that I know more about finding beauty than either truth or right.

For me, the creation of beauty is largely a matter of playing
the piano. I don't play very difficult pieces, just Beatles classics,
favorite songs from musicals, and some familiar classical
works with simple arrangements. And I never perform for
others. I like to play when nobody's around. But if my wife
and children are around, I use the pedal that mutes the sound
so they can decide whether to sit close enough to the piano
to hear the dampened music.

If I had a gift for music, perhaps I'd feel obligated to share
my talent. But thankfully, I am not gifted. So I don't play for
others. I make music for myself. I can create moments of

beauty—at least for a few measures when everything comes together. This much I've come to know: The real meaning of our search for beauty, truth, and right lies not in public performance but in quiet moments when nobody is listening. And if we are in a position to share what we've learned, it is best to do so while using the damper pedal, allowing others to choose whether they wish to draw close and listen.

Futility Refuted

There is no such thing as a lasting peace, a tranquility that will persist forever, a final resting place for the lion and the lamb. We yearn for the completion of our task, the fulfillment of our striving, the consummation of our journey. And this longing sows the seeds of our defeat. We aspire to solve conflicts, we ache to be done with the hard work of life, we pine for the day in which an everlasting peace prevails. In believing that the purpose of a peace movement lies in securing an outcome, in reaching an amicable conclusion, in attaining a serene world, we assure our own frustration, our own futility, and ultimately our own failure.

The work of peacemaking will never be done; that is the curse and the blessing of being human. It's a curse in that there is no utopian culmination of our labors, a blessing in that we will always have meaningful work. The peacemaker is like Sisyphus, whom the gods condemned to an eternal life of shoving a boulder up a hill, only to see it roll back down again in an endless cycle of apparent futility. How could Sisyphus endure such a fate? I've asked my students, and their answers were revealing.

Some students supposed that there is always hope, a hope that the gods will relent, that peace will finally come to Sisyphus and perhaps to us. A particularly creative student suggested that over time, the rolling of the boulder would erode the hill so that eventually the labor of Sisyphus would be complete. Maybe as we roll the boulder of peace in every generation, the hill of hate is worn down. But I believe that the most compelling answer came from those students who understood that a sense of futility comes from the belief that we rightfully expect to see the fruit of our labors. We forget that virtue lies in the doing of good works, not in the completing of our task.

Maybe Sisyphus will never recover the graces of the gods; maybe the hill will never be worn down. But if he—if we— can authentically and deeply engage in our labors, if we roll the boulder of peace because it is what we are called to do, if the measure of our work is its capacity to shape who we are, we can go on pushing. And if in the course of our labors the hill of hate is eroded, that will be a beautiful thing, a very beautiful thing.

But as much as we hope that peacemaking will replace war-mongering, as much as we hope to live at a critical point in human history, as much as we dream of a glorious conversion of society, we must understand that while epiphanies may change souls, they rarely change the world. To know what we can do, to understand what the world needs of us, we must look into the eyes of the frightened soldier and the terrified child. But to sustain our work, we must look inside ourselves. There we shall find the understanding that the endless labor of life is not about changing the world but about creating ourselves. We cannot make the world peaceful, but neither can the world make us hopeless.

Of Pigs and Love

When I was growing up, my family was not much into hugging, crying, or kissing. My parents were from New England and they exemplified Yankee practicality and reserve. It's not that life was barren, but feelings were expressed obliquely.

My dad let me know that I was loved, particularly when I was least lovable. Discovering that I'd done something a tad misguided or just plain stupid, he would look sternly at the disaster, sigh, and mutter, "I should've raised pigs. At least I'd have had something to eat." He was telling me that he'd had children not to provide him with material satisfaction but to bring him joy—even in our blunders. In fact I think he cherished our follies, for these were the moments when he knew most clearly that we had much to learn, and we knew he had much to teach.

Even when my parents' meaning was unambiguous, the communication was indirect. I recall several times finding a carefully folded scrap of paper tucked into my lunch box or coat pocket. My mom simply wrote "I love you" and placed the note where I'd find it without the embarrassment of my classmates' seeing it. These messages appeared at all the right times, like when other kids had been cruel or I was feeling insecure. Raised to be reticent about such matters, I did my best to hide my distress. But somehow Mom knew when I needed to be reminded of her love.

I sort of envy the huggers, criers, and kissers of the world. But in families like mine, quiet expressions of love were not lost amid an endless stream of embraces, tears, and lips. So if you're like me, write, "I love you" on a scrap of paper. Then send it to the person whose follies fail to undermine your deep affection, to someone who is infinitely more valuable to you than pork chops.

Mundane Mediums

乄

The world is in desperate need of shamans, but rather than emissaries of the immaterial realm, I mean the living bridges between human lives—Jews who can speak with Arabs, liberals who can communicate with conservatives, chemists who can converse with poets, and aging feminists who can relate to teenage boys. I mean modern shamans.

Traditional shamans live at the edge of a village, spanning the gap between human and nonhuman worlds. This physical location embodies their deeper purpose. As noted by the philosopher and anthropologist, David Abrams, "The magician's intelligence is not encompassed *within* the society; its place is at the edge of the community, mediating *between* the human community and the beings upon which the village depends for its nourishment and sustenance." In the modern world, people find themselves abutting—and depending on—beings that seem every bit as unfathomable as panthers or poisonwood. Except that these other creatures are also humans.

For my part, I'm an academic shaman. As a "professor of natural sciences and humanities," my task is to bridge the yawning gap between these ways of knowing. I afflict agriculture students with notions of human justice and animal welfare, and English students with contentions that one must know science to write well about nature. Creating dialogue within a university might seem rather mundane, somewhat beneath a genuine shaman's proper work. But the villages of the sciences and humanities have each erected bulwarks of terms, techniques, and traditions. This would be fine except that the problems of the world are too urgent, education too important, and students too valuable for such provincialism.

Many a shadowy presence lurks in the twilight between our modern villages and the larger society. Ignorance is transformed into fear as we ascribe dark, malevolent intentions to those we do not understand. And there are few shamans to guide us—or at least few who have taken on this desperately needed role. Who will guide us into the worlds of the homeless, the religious fundamentalist, the immigrant, the learning disabled, or the schizophrenic? Do you know the world of war veterans, octogenarians, Moslems, AIDS victims, or inner-city youth? Can you show us the world of the paraplegic, atheist, ex-con, or drug addict? We need shamans if we are to understand, if we are to live as neighbors. We need compassionate and courageous guides who can both teach us about them and tell them about us, so that our differences become a source of wonder rather than fear.

Abrams suggested that a shaman has "the ability to readily slip out of the perceptual boundaries that demarcate his or her particular culture . . . in order to make contact with, and learn from the other powers." He was referring to natural powers, and we still have a great deal to learn from crows, forest fires, spring rains, locusts, apples, tsunamis, redwoods, and droughts. But as our village has grown, we no longer border only the natural world—as vital as it is to our nourishment and sustenance. In the dusk we now see other forms, not with tails and branches but with turbans and burkhas. Let us once again seek and heed the wisdom of the shamans.

Better yet, let us become shamans.

A Mother's Socks

Once upon a time, a thief snuck into the room of a sleeping Buddhist monk. As the burglar rummaged about, the monk awoke. The startled thief ran into the snowy streets with the monk racing after him. "Please stop!" the monk called, and the man finally did, realizing that his pursuer was no threat. "You'll need this," the monk gasped, handing the thief his own coat.

"What do you mean?" the man asked.

"I saw that you dashed from my room into the cold without so much as a winter wrap, and I realized that I had both a woolen blanket and a coat."

Having heard this implausible tale of sainthood years ago, I forgot the details but remembered the essential events. Ordinary people can't be morally compelled to make such extraordinary sacrifices. But for whatever reason—perhaps the sheer absurdity of such unconditional altruism—this parable stuck with me. It rattled around in my skeptical mind until the day my wife played the role of the Buddhist monk.

Nan and I had headed into the mountains for a day of skiing with our children, who were four and six at the time. In the chaos of packing up that morning, we'd forgotten our daughter's mittens. The wind was whipping and the mercury hovered in the teens, so no mittens meant no skiing. But for

Nan the solution was as obvious as it was simple. She always wore two pairs of socks, so she removed the outer layer and pulled them over Erin's hands. The problem solved, we headed down the trail.

I found her approach rather clever, the sort of practical, motherly thinking that often eludes my analytical mind, but hardly heroic. However, the bitter cold and the woolen warmth evoked the parable of the monk's coat. Among the snow-hushed pines, I remembered how the dialogue ended:

"I don't understand," the man said.

"It is simple. You have nothing at all to keep you warm," the monk answered.

"But you are a fool to give away your coat, leaving you with only a blanket," the man replied, reaching for the garment.

"If I had two gloves on one hand and none on the other, would I be a fool to put one of them on my bare hand?" the monk asked.

The man said nothing, took the coat, and hurried down the street.

When we are not alienated, when love draws us into the suffering of others, when we see our happiness entwined in their well-being, then generosity is neither foolish nor heroic. It is the simplest and most obvious choice.

Pocket Watch Rebellion

I loaned my watch to my son and he broke it—for which I am now deeply thankful, although my initial reaction was admittedly not gratitude. Ethan was contrite, but he probably suspected that a plastic digital watch didn't represent a major financial loss. It did, however, have great sentimental value. My parents gave it to me nearly twenty years ago, when I needed a cheap but rugged timepiece for my first year of field ecology in Wyoming. And to be fair, Ethan didn't break the working part of the watch, he broke the gizmo that joins the band to the watch. So it still tells time, but I can't wear it. And that is a blessing.

I'd worn a watch since I was a kid. My first watch was a silvery Timex with hour and minute hands. I had never questioned the convenience and practicality of being able to know the time at a glance. This perceived necessity for instant access to the time came into conflict with my emotional attachment to the broken watch. I couldn't just throw it out; not only had it become a part of my story but it still worked. So I converted it into a pocket watch.

Half of the watchband was still firmly attached, and I was able to affix it to my keychain, which is always in my pocket. I still had easy access to my watch, although it no longer stared up from my wrist. This small change, moving the watch from center stage to the wings, had a subtle but remarkably pervasive effect.

To check the time, I had to reach into my pocket and pull out the watch—which made me keenly aware of how much the clock had become an organizing tyrant. During conversations with people at work, I typically peeked at my watch as if it were an overseer scowling at me for socializing instead of working. I'd often check my watch to measure progress on a project ("Geez, only a page of writing in the last fifty-three minutes"). My watch had become the mediator of my life, like the center line that a driver unthinkingly tracks to be sure he's on course.

With my watch tucked away, time is no longer the motif of my days. Of course, I check my watch when I know that I'm due at a meeting, and I set the alarm to make sure I don't miss appointments, but these are conscious, intentional acts. During a discussion with a student, I'll catch myself starting to glance downward out of habit. Then I'll smile inwardly, for my hairy wrist is a living structure, an organic, pulsing part of me rather than a strapped-on chunk of technology. And I realize that relationship, not efficiency, is at the core of life.

Owning a broken watch hasn't magically transformed me into a fully aware person. But it has been a wonderful gift from my parents—and my son. At least I feel a bit liberated, with time no longer quite the taskmaster it used to be. And I've not missed an important event or been late to an essential engagement. Two or three times a day, my watch reminds me that I should be somewhere else, but most of the time I really need to be right here and now.

Life Preservers

Melody—one of the sweetest, kindest, gentlest women I've known—suffered terribly. Because of me. Her profound distress was difficult to watch, both because she was such a decent person and because I was the source of her pain. Melody was a student assigned to help me in my graduate school research. While engaged in the repetitive, mundane tasks that so often go into science, we'd shared our views of the world. And in this way she came to discover that I had not been saved.

As a devout Christian, she felt obligated to do everything in her power to bring others into the fold. But I was not just another heathen; I'd become a friend, so her sense of duty was even more compelling. She was nearly desperate to keep me from walking into the fires of hell. And the impending spiritual disaster was made all the more tragic because I had consciously chosen the path to perdition.

Melody invited me to lunchtime Bible studies, which I gently declined. Finally, I felt so bad about her anxiety for my fate that I went along. But it was like throwing a life preserver to a drowning man who refuses to grab the ring because he thinks he's out for a pleasant swim. I know she prayed fervently for me, and I wished sincerely for her happiness. In the end, she graduated and married a fine young man. So it seems that at least my wish was granted, although I suspect she did not soon forget her drowning friend.

I've often been in Melody's position. As a professor, I have spent a great deal of energy trying to convert other people. There was the lazy but gifted student whom I wanted to turn into a scholar, the arrogant colleague I wanted to turn into a doubter, and the cynical administrator I wanted to turn into an idealist. Outside work, there was the miserly member of my church I wanted to turn into a generous giver, the despairing friend I wanted to turn into an optimist, and the happy-go-lucky fellow I wanted to turn into a realist. But they all, to a person, refused to reach out for my life preserver. Some even seemed happy while the pounding surf of mistaken perceptions and the crashing waves of unrealized potential washed over them. I agonized over their fate and lamented their failings. I suffered for them.

At least I suffered until I finally realized that I was trying to convert the wrong person. The essence of happiness lies not in changing colleagues into people I can respect, students into people I can value, or friends into people I can love. The task is instead to turn myself into a person who can respect, value, and love others. I'm still working on it, so I still feel compelled to save others on occasion.

But at least now when I attempt a rescue, I don't stand on the deck of my ship and throw a flotation device. I jump in after them. That way I begin to understand that treading water on your own can be more meaingful than wearing someone else's life jacket. What appears to be drowning may just be a pleasant swim. And sometimes I find that being tossed by their waves is preferable to the navigational certainty aboard my ship.

Go Fly a Kite

Wind has a dark power over us, the capacity to trigger depression, despondency, and even—according to eighteenth-century physicians—madness. How is it that moving air, an invisible presence, can so deeply disturb the human psyche? We have created our own vulnerability. In an age of technological hubris, we must confront the realization that the wind is absolutely uncontrollable.

The wind is a wild beast with no regard for our rationality. It mauls our sense of dominion. Umbrellas keep us dry, moisturizers keep us wet, silk keeps us cool, wool keeps us warm, creams keep us from burning, but nothing vanquishes the wind. Those who are determined to dominate the world are antagonized by the wind. But those who accept the untamed forces of nature avoid such frustrations. And it is possible then to move from a mere defense of our sanity to genuine flourishing.

To be sane, embrace the wind. But to be joyous, fly a kite. Dance between caprice and control. The wind pulls the fragile sail upward and the flyer plays out the string. Left to the turbulence, the kite will be dashed to the ground or swept over the horizon. Left on the ground, the kite is moribund, stagnant. But between sky and earth is enchantment.

We are kites, buffeted by the vicissitudes of the spirit, the squalls of fortune, the breezes of intuition, and the glorious

gusts of chance encounters. And we are stabilized by a tail—
the solidity of the mind, the bedrock of reason, the granite of
science. If our tail is too heavy, we never leave the ground. If
it is too light, we spin crazily.

The people in our lives—family, lovers, friends, community
—are the braided strands, a kite string that sustains the dynamic
tension between heaven and earth. They are a lifeline that
allows us to be uplifted, to see farther, to live more fully.
And the higher we fly, the stronger our string must be. For
when our connection becomes worn and frayed it can snap,
and we will come tumbling back to the earth, landing far
from where we left, with nobody to repair our breaks or
mend our tears.

And so rejoice in the wind—but attend to your string.

The Majority

In Rome a million people marched; in London a hundred thousand; in New York City fifty thousand. On a bitterly cold day in late March, seventeen intrepid souls (counting the three dogs) gathered at a city park in Laramie, Wyoming, to mount a protest against the war in Iraq.

When a young woman at the rally was asked by a reporter, "What can so few people hope to accomplish?" she replied with a sweep of her arm. The skeptical journalist cocked a graying eyebrow.

"What do you see?" she asked. A vacant bandshell rose against the somber sky as if to mock the half-circle of protestors facing a speaker whose words were swept away by a sleety wind.

He didn't reply.

"Nothing," she offered, answering her own question. "There's nobody here but us. No people celebrating violence. Nobody supporting the war. Just us."

He scribbled a few notes about what he considered a quixotic gathering. When his pen paused, she went on.

"Today," she offered, "we are the majority in this democracy. Our voices may be few, but they are infinitely louder than silence."

He looked at her paternalistically, letting her know that she was sweet but wholly naive. His condescending smile invited her to provide a final sound bite for the story.

"We aren't here just to be nice," she offered tensely. Then she gathered herself. "We came together because it matters." Her voice tailed off to a whisper, revealing a mixture of deep authenticity and profound disappointment.

The reporter jotted a few more notes and scurried to his car. The story never appeared in the paper. It would have been nice, but it didn't matter.

Acknowledgments

No life, let alone a set of writings about life, finds meaning in isolation. I would like to thank those friends who read an early draft of these meditations and offered their insights: Karen Bartsch, David Estes, Linda Goldman, Jeremy Page, Bill and Norma Reiners, and Jen Wright. I must also express my deepest gratitude and love to my wife, Nan, and my children, Erin and Ethan, for their support, inspiration, and permission to tell stories of our family. And I offer my profound thanks to Mary Benard, who knows that editing is like ministry and was able to offer comfort and affliction in just the right doses.

Unitarian Universalist Meditation Manuals

❧

Unitarians and Universalists have been publishing prayer collections and meditation manuals for 150 years. In 1841 the Unitarians broke with their tradition of addressing only theological topics and published *Short Prayers for the Morning and Evening of Every Day in the Week, with Occasional Prayers and Thanksgivings*. Over the years, the Unitarians published many more volumes of prayers, including Theodore Parker's selections. In 1938 *Gaining a Radiant Faith* by Henry H. Saunderson launched the tradition of an annual Lenten manual.

Several Universalist collections appeared in the early nineteenth century. A comprehensive *Book of Prayers* was published in 1839, featuring both public and private devotions. Like the Unitarians, the Universalists published Lenten manuals, and in the 1950s they complemented this series with Advent manuals.

Since 1961, the year the Unitarians and Universalists consolidated, the Lenten manual has evolved into a meditation manual.